The Healing of Harms

Destiny Parsons

Published by Destiny Parsons, 2025.

While every precaution has been taken in the preparation of this book, the publisher assumes no responsibility for errors or omissions, or for damages resulting from the use of the information contained herein.

THE HEALING OF HARMS

First edition. May 9, 2025.

Copyright © 2025 Destiny Parsons.

ISBN: 979-8218675899

Written by Destiny Parsons.

Table of Contents

Chapter One: 1
Chapter Two: 4
Chapter Three: 6
Chapter Four: 8
Chapter Five: 10
Chapter Six: 12
Chapter Seven: 14
Chapter Eight: 17
Chapter Nine: 19
Chapter Ten: 21
Chapter Eleven: 23
Chapter Twelve: 26
Chapter Thirteen: 28
Chapter Fourteen: 30
Chapter Fifteen: 32
Chapter Sixteen: 35
Chapter Seventeen: 36
Chapter Eighteen: 37
Chapter Nineteen: 39
Chapter Twenty: 41
Chapter Twenty-One: 42
Chapter Twenty-Two: 44
Chapter Twenty-Three: 46
Chapter Twenty-Four: 48
Chapter Twenty-Five: 50
Chapter Twenty-Six: 53
Chapter Twenty-Seven: 57
Chapter Twenty-Eight: 59
Chapter Twenty-Nine: 61
Chapter Thirty: 64
Chapter Thirty-One: 67
Chapter Thirty-Two: 69
Chapter Thirty-Three: 71

Chapter Thirty-Four: 73
Chapter Thirty-Five: 76
Chapter Thirty-Six: 78
Chapter Thirty-Seven: 80
Chapter Thirty-Eight: 83
Chapter Thirty-Nine: 86
Chapter Forty: 88
Chapter Forty-One: 91

To my daughter,

The light in my darkest moments,

the purpose in my pain,

and the reason I kept pressing forward when everything said quit.

You are the spark that lit my fight,

the melody behind my voice,

and the miracle I've had the honor to witness unfold.

This book is for you.

May you always know how loved you are,

how fiercely you were fought for,

and how deeply your life matters.

To those who have ever felt unseen, unworthy, or

unqualified—

This is your reminder:

God uses the broken to build the beautiful.

Chapter One:

"The Climb"

This has never been a story about ease—it's about the climb. The long, steep, exhausting climb. The kind that tests your lungs, your heart, and your will to keep going. There were seasons I wanted to stop walking, times I was gasping for breath through sobs nobody saw. But somehow, step by step, God kept lifting me.

The climb wasn't just uphill—it was through thorns, over broken glass, with burdens I didn't think I could carry. Shame. Regret. Loss. Being misunderstood. Sleepless nights in a car while others said, "Be safe," never knowing the real danger was the weight I carried inside.

But there was also beauty in the climb. Because that's where I found my strength. That's where I found my voice. And that's where I found God.

Each step showed me something. Sometimes, He let me crawl. Sometimes, He carried me. But He never left me.

This climb was never about a finish line—it was about becoming. And with every step, I discovered a version of me I didn't know existed. One that wasn't afraid of the dark anymore. One that could write books, sing songs, love harder, and stand taller—no matter what they said about me.

This is still a climb. But now, I've got joy in the struggle. I've got perspective in the pain. And I know with everything in me: what God is building at the top is worth every aching step.

I've always been a relationship girl. Looking back, I realize I rarely stayed single for long—and when I did commit, it was for years at a time. Five years was usually the minimum. But even in what many would call a mistake, I've found deep gratitude.

My last relationship, back in 2013, was abusive. And yet, I say with complete honesty—I am grateful. That chapter of my life humbled me in a way nothing else could. It reshaped my heart. The kind of pain I endured then softened me, made me more compassionate toward others. I feel things deeply, sometimes I feel I do too much, but I'm learning how to manage that sensitivity as a strength, not a weakness—with God's help, of course. But it also taught me how to let Him handle those who mishandle me.

What I thank God for most is that my daughter never knew that man on any real level. She was spared. Completely untouched by that part of my life, and I see now that it was only by God's hand. Her innocence is still intact, and that alone was worth every sacrifice. I made the hardest choice a mother could make—to step back so she wouldn't have to suffer, to shield her from bouncing between instability and pain.

She has never seen another man around me. And she won't. Not until I'm absolutely sure he's the one. Because she deserves to see what real love looks like—not what I had to survive, or someone coming in and out of her life.

There was a time when her question, "When can I come live with you, Mom?" used to crush me. I'd carry the weight of it for days. I wanted so badly to say, "Right now. Let's go home." But the truth was, I didn't have a home yet—not the kind she deserved. The one time I did have a place, she knew deep down it wasn't really mine. It was a man's house—someone who helped me, yes, but still not ours.

Now, by the grace of God, that question doesn't hold the same power over me. It doesn't sting like it used to. Not because I care less, but because I trust more. I've grown. I've healed. I know God's timing is perfect, and He's preparing the kind of home we both can be proud of—built not just with walls, but with wisdom, peace, and true stability.

There were days I'd drop her off and feel like my soul had been ripped out. I'd drive away screaming at the top of my lungs, tears blurring my vision, not even caring if anyone saw. By the time I hit the stop sign, I was begging God to take me—praying I'd drive off the side of the mountain and the pain would end. That's how deep it cut. That's how heavy the ache was.

But even then, He held me. Even when I didn't want to be held. Even when I couldn't see past the grief, the guilt, the hopelessness—He was there. And I'm here. Still breathing. Still rising. That stop sign didn't stop me—it became the start of something new.

Here's the kicker—how does a mother just move on and build a life, start a new family, when her daughter still asks when she can come home? When she still longs to be part of that "family" you're trying to build?

How do you dream about new beginnings while knowing the one person who should be sitting at the table still doesn't have a seat? How do you go on when the worst has already happened? It's a question that never stops echoing in the quiet moments. No matter how much healing I chase, how many blessings come, there's always a piece of my heart sitting in the backseat asking, "When, Mom? When do I get to come with you?"

And the truth? I don't have all the answers. But I'm trusting the One who does.

I wasn't a saint, and I don't want anyone to read this and think otherwise. There were seasons where I had a death wish. I sold my prescriptions, made reckless choices, and truthfully, it's only by the grace of God that I never ended up in prison. I've done things that still make me shake my head, but now—now I'm choosing a different path. A new mindset. A new direction. One I've never seen modeled around me. I don't crave the numbness like I used to. In fact, I'm terrified to lose the still, quiet voice of the Holy Spirit. Whether it's alcohol, pills, or anything else that clouds my judgment—I want no part of it.

The Spirit is gentle. If you're not tuned in, it's too easy to talk yourself out of what He clearly said. But then something happens. A vision unfolds, a promise shows up in a way that only God could have orchestrated—and you know. You know it was Him.

I've been building toward something for what feels like sixteen years. At first, my goal was to have my daughter back before her father got out of prison. When that didn't happen, I told myself—by eighteen, she'll choose for herself. But then came the brain surgery. And now, I have to hold on to hope. I have to believe first. Because healing takes time. And freedom—real freedom—begins with faith.

Father God, thank You that I am made free.

Chapter Two:

"The Flower in Bloom"

Some stories begin with comfort. Mine began with fire. Not the kind that warms, but the kind that refines. I wasn't an orphan by definition, but I often felt like one. I had both birth parents, yet the house never truly felt like home. When the storms came, there wasn't a safe place to run back to. If an emergency ever happened, walking through my parents' door simply wasn't an option. And that does something to a child.

I was raised with both parents until they separated when I was about five or six. I lived with my mother until I was sixteen, and then moved in with my father—a man I loved deeply, who felt more like a friend than a parent. A few months after my eighteenth birthday, he died from a heroin overdose. That loss marked the beginning of a survival season I wasn't ready for. There was nowhere to go, no one to catch me. That's the year I started dancing topless for money. What began as a dare with friends turned into the only option I could see.

I was working two jobs from sun up to sun down and still couldn't afford a place of my own. The void left from not having strong bonds with my family made me crave identity in places that couldn't offer it. My mother was kind, gentle, but burdened with guilt and grief that I didn't understand until I carried some of it myself. She blamed herself for things out of her control, and I learned early how heavy shame can feel, even when it isn't yours.

We weren't a "church on Sunday" kind of family, though we believed in God. But the kind of belief that doesn't go deep—it doesn't transform you. Not like it has for me now. Not like the way God would later grip my life and show me that I was never invisible to Him.

There were days I laughed too loud or spilled a glass of milk, and the disapproval in my stepfather's voice could freeze me in place. We would walk on eggshells, tiptoeing around. Unable to grab ice from the ice maker, things were very strict. My sibling and I would barricade ourselves in the rooms to keep things peaceful and avoid being verbally attacked because of something we did or didn't do the way it should have been done. And when we did get out of the house, we would have to be let off up the road and walk the rest of the way home. Not having a healthy and functional relationship with my real father made me resent my stepfather at times. Even though, now I know it kept me out of trouble and harm's way. We have a much better relationship now that I am older.

My relationship with my real father was tender, but complicated. He was loved by everyone, but I loved him with something deeper—a daughter's longing to be seen by her father. I looked like him. I wanted to know him more. And just like that, he was gone. Leaving me with questions, trauma, and a soul that needed more than survival.

Looking back, I now see how God had His hand on me even in my rebellion, even in the places I thought He would never follow me into. I didn't want fame. I just wanted my daughter to see me on TV and recognize me—to know that I was still trying, still alive, still fighting for her.

This book is not just about the pain. It's about how God can use every shattered thing to create something whole. It's not about being perfect—it's about being present. And from this first chapter, I want you to know—there is a way out of the fire. Not just to survive it, but to come out of it glowing.

Chapter Three:

"Grew Wings from the Stings and Broken Things"

There are some lessons you don't learn until the fall. Until the night is cold, and your body is aching from another night sleeping in your car. Until you've heard "be safe" so many times it starts to sound like a warning and a whisper of what could go wrong—but you're already living in what did.

See, people don't always understand that the boogeyman you fear most isn't out there. It's the voices in your head, the memories that replay, the ache of watching your child drive away while you sit at a stop sign screaming into the silence. That was me, praying I could just drive off the edge and be done. But God wouldn't let go. Not even then.

I've had men at my window while I slept—no sound, just a holy stirring in my spirit that jolted me awake just in time to protect myself. I've opened my eyes to someone rummaging through my car, completely unaware I was in the back seat. I've laughed through fear and sweat through nights so cold they felt like punishment—but somehow, even in all of it, there was still grace. Because I survived.

I'm not a saint. I had a death wish. I sold pills. I made choices I shouldn't have. But I never ended up in prison, and that's not because I was clever—it's because God had a plan that the enemy couldn't abort. I should've been another statistic. But I wasn't. Not by chance. By grace.

My daughter, Nevaeh, still asks when she can come live with me. And I still have to tell her, "Mom doesn't have a home yet. Not the kind you deserve." The one home she remembers—the man's house that let me stay—wasn't ours. It was a borrowed chapter. Not the ending I prayed for.

And yet... God. He's been teaching me that His goodness doesn't expire. That the fruit from this season will last. That just because it hurts doesn't mean it's hopeless. I've changed. I don't numb the pain like I used to. I don't crave the same things. I fear anything that clouds my mind because I crave His Spirit more than comfort now. And His voice? It's quiet. It's a whisper that you can miss if you're not listening.

I've built for sixteen years. The goal was to get her back before her dad finished his sentence. That didn't happen. Then it was by the time she turned 18. But brain surgery changed everything. So now—I believe. And I wait. Because God's timing may feel slow, but it's always right.

I have lived through losses that should have broken me. But they didn't. They bloomed something new. From every sting, every betrayal, every pit—I grew wings.

So no, this chapter isn't about pain. It's about flight. About learning to soar after the fall. And I believe—if you're reading this—you can too.

Chapter Four:

"The Beauty of Becoming"

Healing doesn't always look like glowing skin, peaceful mornings, and gentle prayers. Sometimes it looks like holding your breath at the gas station because you're $3 short and hoping the car starts. Sometimes, healing is a war zone in your mind where the loudest voice is your doubt, and you've got to learn to silence it with faith.

Becoming isn't easy.

This chapter—the in-between—is where many give up. And I almost did. After all, what's the point of a race if your child turns 18 before she can come home? What's the point of all this praying, hoping, building, waiting... if the finish line keeps moving?

But then God whispered, "The goal was never just to get her back. The goal was for you to become."

And I wept.

Because it's true. I was so focused on proving I was a good mother, a stable mother, a restored mother—that I missed the miracle of being remade in the process. God wasn't just building a life for me to hand over to my daughter. He was building a woman who could lead her.

I've grown to understand that I wasn't rejected—I was preserved. Protected from environments that would've kept me bound, from people who didn't value the God in me. I've been misunderstood, dismissed, labeled—but never forsaken. Even on the nights I screamed into the steering wheel, God held me close.

And now? Now I'm becoming.

I'm becoming someone who no longer chases validation. Someone who doesn't need a man's house or a platform to prove her worth. Someone who's okay with starting over, again and again, if it means being in God's will. Someone who understands that love doesn't compete—it covers. That parenting isn't about perfection—it's about presence.

I used to think healing would come in a perfect house with a perfect job and my daughter under my roof. But healing came in the process. In the trenches. In the car. In the gym showers. In between auditions. Healing came when I said, "Even if this doesn't look like what I prayed for, I'll trust You anyway."

That's the beauty of becoming.

Not everything's fixed. But everything's different. I'm not who I was. And for that—I praise Him.

Chapter Five:

"Heaven's Lessons in the Hard Places"

There are some lessons that only come through pain. Not because God wants us to suffer, but because suffering softens the soil. You can't grow fruit in hard, untouched ground. And my heart—it used to be stone.

But the hard places taught me how to bend. They taught me how to feel, how to listen, and most importantly, how to lean into the Father when the world felt too heavy.

I used to be a fighter in the wrong ways. Loud. Angry. Hardened. I fought to be heard. I fought to be loved. I fought to prove I mattered. But God... He started teaching me how to fight differently. Not with fists or fear—but with faith. Not with bitterness—but with boundaries.

There were nights I laid in my car with tears soaking into my pillow and whispered, "God, are You still here? What's my purpose here?" And somehow, even in the silence, I knew He was. He didn't always answer how I wanted. But He answered. Sometimes in the form of a stranger offering a helping hand. Sometimes through the kindness of a nurse. Sometimes with a check in the mail I wasn't expecting. But always, in just enough time.

God was pruning me. He was stripping away the pride, the false strength, the need to always have it together. And what He revealed underneath was someone I didn't recognize—but someone I'm learning to love. A woman who's honest about her flaws. A mother who shows up even when she feels invisible. A daughter who has learned to sit at the feet of her Father when she doesn't have the answers.

I've had to unlearn survival. I've had to stop waiting for the next attack and start preparing for the blessing. Because the enemy doesn't fight what isn't a threat—and he came for me hard. But God... He came harder.

This chapter of my life is less about proving myself and more about trusting Him. I don't have to earn the promise. I just have to obey.

So I wake up. I show up. I worship. I write. I forgive. I walk away from what wounds me. I set the table in faith, even if I don't see the feast yet.

Because the lesson of the hard place is this: even here, God is good. Even here, I am growing. Even here, I am not alone.

Chapter Six:

"Made for More"

I used to think surviving was enough—if I could just make it through the day, if I could just push through the pain, maybe that was all life had for me. But somewhere in the quiet moments with God, I realized something deep down in my spirit: I wasn't made just to survive.

I was made for more.

More than the trauma that tried to claim me.

More than the labels that tried to define me.

More than the mistakes I made when I was lost and desperate for love.

I was made to thrive. To shine. To soar.

But before I could step into "more," I had to let go of what I thought I was. The dancer. The damaged. The doubted. I had to surrender my need to control the timing and trust the One who made time itself.

God started showing me glimpses—visions of purpose, of restoration, of legacy. Not just for me, but for my daughter. For the people who would one day read these words. For the ones who felt like giving up but didn't.

I remember sitting in my car one night—cold, tired, hungry—but my spirit stirred. God whispered, You are not forgotten. And that voice... it shook something loose in me. It reminded me that this world doesn't define my worth—He does.

He reminded me that every time I gave instead of took, every time I forgave instead of fought back, every time I spoke life over myself when I felt dead inside—I was planting seeds. And those seeds were growing.

I may not have had a house, but I had peace.

I may not have had money, but I had favor.

I may not have had certainty, but I had vision.

And that was enough to take one more step.

This is the season of knowing who I am—really knowing. Not just from what I've been through, but from who created me. This is the chapter where I stop apologizing for being chosen. This is the chapter where I trade shame for strength. Where I stop proving and start praising.

I was made for more—and now, I'm walking in it.

Chapter Seven:

"Breaking Cycles, Building Legacy"

Every chain has a sound when it hits the ground. I've heard mine fall—one by one—as I began to follow the voice of the One who called me out.

Generational pain ran deep through my bloodline, but the Spirit of God ran deeper. What was normal in my family—the silence, the secrets, the survival—stopped feeling like "home" when I met truth. Once I tasted freedom, I couldn't go back.

This chapter is about doing things differently, even if it means doing it scared.

Even if it means doing it alone.

When I was little, I didn't know what legacy meant. Now I know it's everything.

It's not what I leave behind—it's what I build right now.

I started breaking cycles not by being perfect but by being willing—willing to be misunderstood, willing to walk away from dysfunction, willing to say, "This stops with me."

And sometimes... willing to cry through it, pray through it, praise through it.

I've learned to make decisions that my daughter will benefit from even if she doesn't see it yet. I've learned to walk away from places where I felt small, even if it meant I had to sleep in my car just to protect my peace. I've learned to speak life, even when my own breath felt shallow.

What I'm building is quiet right now, but it's sacred.

It's not for applause—it's for legacy.

It's not built with money—it's built with obedience.

And I know one thing for sure: when God builds it, it can't be shaken.

King James Version (KJV):
"But the mercy of the Lord is from everlasting to everlasting upon them that fear him, and his righteousness unto children's children;"
Psalms 103:17-18 (KJV)

Chapter Eight:

"The Mercy That Met Me"

There's a certain kind of mercy that follows you even when you think you've run too far to be caught. I've felt it. When I had nothing left, when the prayers were silent cries that only my soul could hear, mercy showed up. I didn't earn it. I didn't feel worthy of it. But God covered me anyway.

This chapter of my life wasn't wrapped in pretty paper. It was raw, gritty, and tangled with moments where I questioned everything. Yet somehow, He kept showing up—gently but powerfully. He didn't just rescue me—He renewed me. He started cleaning up the mess I didn't know how to untangle.

I look back at times where I should've been dead—physically, emotionally, and spiritually. And I realize now, mercy walked into rooms before I ever did. Mercy stood between me and the cliff's edge. It rode shotgun in my car when I didn't know where I was going. It tucked me in when I slept freezing in my backseat. That mercy? It had no expiration date. It had no conditions. It simply was.

I used to think I had to earn grace—prove myself. But the truth is, I only had to receive it. I think about my daughter and how much she has endured, and I realize... she's covered too. The Word says God's righteousness extends to children's children. That means the same mercy that met me in my lowest moment is now flowing through my bloodline, through hers, and through every prayer I've ever whispered over her in secret.

This mercy isn't weak—it's fierce. It defends, it restores, and it silences every voice that said we were too far gone. It broke cycles. It changed stories. It gave me breath when I didn't even want to breathe anymore.

And now? Now I see that mercy not only held me, it's sending me. I'm walking proof that His love has no limits, no conditions, and no distance too great. This chapter is just the beginning of understanding the power of being chosen—not because I'm perfect, but because He is.

King James Version (KJV):
"Thou hast enlarged my steps under me, that my feet did not slip."
Psalm 18:36 (KJV)

Chapter Nine:

"Grace in the Grit"

There's something powerful about getting up when no one else knows you fell. This chapter—this season—wasn't about dramatic announcements or rescue missions. It was about quiet endurance. About living in the in-between. It was the season where I wasn't where I used to be, but I also hadn't yet arrived. I was "somewhere in the middle," and the middle is where faith is forged.

By this point, I had experienced losses that could've made me bitter, but God was teaching me to become better. I wasn't dancing anymore. I wasn't running from pain anymore. I was trying to walk through it—head up, hands open. My daughter's surgery had changed everything. Her healing became a picture of my own. Watching her re-learn life taught me how to live mine differently. We were both starting over, just in different ways.

The biggest difference? She didn't choose her starting over. But I had to choose mine—daily.

Some nights, I'd sleep in my car, freezing cold or sweating through a summer night, wondering if this sacrifice would ever be worth it. I wasn't chasing fame. I wasn't trying to impress. I just wanted to build something lasting. Something stable. I wanted a story I could point to and say, "That's what God did."

This chapter was where God introduced me to discipline. I wasn't perfect—I still had moments I wanted to numb out, run back to what was familiar. But I knew I couldn't. I had seen too much. Felt too much. The Spirit had whispered to me, and once you've heard Him, silence is no longer an option.

He began to teach me the power of not reacting. Of pausing before speaking. Of choosing peace even when chaos was offered.

I began to sense that although I hadn't yet seen my harvest, the soil was changing. My roots were deeper. My prayers were different. Less about fixing everything around me, and more about transforming everything within me.

I was still waiting for the home. Still waiting for stability. But I wasn't waiting without purpose.

God doesn't waste the middle. And neither would I.

King James Version (KJV):
"But they that wait upon the Lord shall renew their strength; they shall mount up with wings as eagles;
they shall run, and not be weary;
and they shall walk, and not faint."
Isaiah 40:31 (KJV)

Chapter Ten:

"The Weight and the Wind"

By now, you would think I'd be used to carrying the weight. But some seasons bring a different kind of heaviness. Not the kind that makes you collapse—but the kind that makes you question if you should even keep standing. The kind that presses on your chest while you're smiling in public. The kind that sneaks into your prayers and turns your bold declarations into quiet, weary whispers.

After all the progress, after all the faith, I started asking, "What now?" My daughter had turned 18. The brain surgery was behind us. The goal I had fought for—raising her into adulthood with safety and stability—was technically accomplished. And yet, I didn't feel victorious. I felt exhausted.

The adrenaline of survival was gone, and what remained was silence. Stillness. It didn't feel like peace—it felt like empty.

People celebrated my endurance. They praised my strength. But they didn't see the nights I stared out the window wondering if the race even mattered anymore. They didn't hear me question why I fought so hard if I still felt so alone. What happens when you reach the top of a mountain and realize you're too tired to enjoy the view?

I started to grieve the years I lost. Not because I wanted pity, but because for the first time in a long time, I had space to feel it. I had space to remember that healing takes more than grit—it takes grace. And grace, sometimes, is letting yourself admit you're tired.

But here's the miracle: even in the wind, even under the weight, I was still standing. I hadn't gone back. I hadn't given in. And that—that—is a miracle too.

God reminded me in this chapter that strength doesn't always look like motion. Sometimes it looks like stillness. Like holding your ground. Like not quitting.

I began to realize that just because my "why" had changed didn't mean my purpose had disappeared. Maybe now it wasn't just about getting my daughter back—it was about becoming the kind of woman she could look up to for the rest of her life.

And slowly, the wind began to carry me again. Not in the way it did before, but in a new way. A deeper way. I wasn't flying yet—but I could feel the lift beneath my wings.

King James Version (KJV):
"Let us not be weary in well doing:
for in due season we shall reap,
if we faint not."
Galatians 6:9 (KJV)

Chapter Eleven:

"When the Rain Fell Softly"

There's a moment after the storm passes where the world goes still—not with fear, but with reverence. The kind of quiet where you realize you survived what you thought would destroy you. This chapter was that moment for me.

I remember sitting alone in my car, watching the rain gently tap on the windshield. Not like the violent downpours I'd braved before, but soft—almost like a lullaby from heaven. For the first time in a long time, the chaos around me didn't feel like it was swallowing me. It felt like a baptism. A fresh start.

God was speaking in that soft rain. Whispering promises I had almost forgotten He made.

I had spent years building stability like it was a fortress. Fighting to prove I was worthy of being a mother, a provider, a woman of value. But in that stillness, I started to understand something deeper: I already was.

The battle didn't make me worthy. The resume didn't make me worthy.

He did.

This chapter became less about survival and more about identity. It was the start of realizing I was more than what I had fought through. I was more than my trauma, more than my testimony. I was a child of God. Fully loved. Fully seen. Fully held.

I didn't have all the answers. But I had peace. And in a world like this, peace is a rare and precious jewel.

I started dreaming again—not out of desperation, but out of hope. I started making plans—not to escape, but to build. I wasn't just reacting anymore. I was creating.

That's the power of the soft rain. It doesn't shout. It doesn't demand. But it nourishes the soil that will one day bloom with fruit you forgot you planted.

King James Version (KJV):
"Thou wilt keep him in perfect peace,
whose mind is stayed on thee:
because he trusteth in thee."
Isaiah 26:3 (KJV)

Chapter Twelve:

"The God Who Sees"

I used to think I was invisible. Not because people couldn't see me, but because they never really saw me. They saw the mistakes. They saw the struggle. They saw the headlines, the whispers, the past.

But God—He saw me.

Not the image I tried to maintain. Not the pain I tried to hide. Not even the fight I tried to keep up every day. He saw the scared little girl who just wanted to be chosen. The mother who would have given anything just to hold her baby one more day without fear of losing her again. The woman who had climbed out of hell with scraped knees and a tired heart—but never gave up.

In this chapter, I learned that God isn't distant. He's not up in the sky with a clipboard marking every wrong move. He's right here. In the details. In the decisions. In the detours.

I had come a long way from the girl who danced for dollars to survive. That chapter of my life had been written in sweat and prayers whispered between beats of music. But this chapter—this was different. This was sacred ground.

He showed me favor in ways I didn't understand. Jobs I didn't apply for. People who came out of nowhere to help. An unexpected check. A gentle reminder in the middle of the night that I was not forgotten.

I didn't have to perform anymore. I didn't have to prove myself. I just had to believe that the God who called me was also the God who would finish what He started.

He saw me when I was invisible to everyone else. He saw my tears, my sacrifice, my silence.

And He didn't just see—He responded.

This is the God who sees you, too.

King James Version (KJV):
"Thou art the God that seest me."
Genesis 16:13 (KJV)

Chapter Thirteen:

"Oil from the Crushing"

There's a moment when the crushing becomes too much. When the pressure feels like it's going to break you. And maybe it does—but not in the way you expect. It doesn't break you to destroy you. It breaks you to release something sacred.

Oil.
Purpose.
Anointing.

This chapter of my life felt like a slow grind of everything I thought I had under control. Financial hardship. Emotional exhaustion. The weight of motherhood. The ache of being misunderstood—even by those closest to me. The world told me I was strong, but God was showing me that strength in Him looks a lot different than the version I'd created to survive.

He began to strip away everything I depended on—people, places, performances. He took me back to the bare soil. And just like an olive has to be pressed for oil to flow, I had to be crushed for the power in me to be released.

There were days I didn't want to get out of the car I slept in. Nights when the heat or cold made my skin ache. And then there were moments in the middle of all that suffering when I heard the still, small voice of God whispering, "I'm with you."

When I say He met me in my lowest places—I mean the literal parking lots, backseats, and rest stop bathrooms. When I had nothing to offer but my surrender, He accepted it like an offering of gold.

That's when I realized: the enemy thought the crushing would end me, but it was the very thing God used to anoint me.

There's oil on my life because I didn't die in the pressing. I grew stronger. Softer. Wiser. The pain produced something I never expected—peace.

It wasn't immediate. But it was inevitable. Because when God is in the crushing, there's always a resurrection.

King James Version (KJV):
"But we have this treasure in earthen vessels,
that the excellency of the power may be of God, and not of us."
2 Corinthians 4:7 (KJV)

Chapter Fourteen:

"The Road Wasn't Wasted"

Some roads feel too long. Too twisted. Too bruised by detours and dead ends to ever make sense.

But I've come to understand—nothing is wasted when God is the one guiding your steps. Even the roads I wish I never had to walk... are part of the map He's using to bring me to purpose.

I look back now and see seasons that felt unbearable: nights in my car, rejection from people I loved, relationships that should have destroyed me, and losses I still grieve. But I also see the breadcrumbs God left along the way—reminders I wasn't alone.

I remember crying in my car, staring at the roof, wondering if my daughter would ever fully recover. I remember feeling so low that I couldn't see the point in continuing. I remember the ache of knowing I wasn't welcome in the place I once called home—and the strength it took to keep walking anyway.

But then came the moments I didn't expect:

A role in a film that reminded me I'm more than my pain.

Strangers who became blessings.

A second opinion that saved my daughter's life.

And peace that didn't make sense, but showed up anyway.

God is the only one who can turn survival into testimony. The very places I wept became the soil where new strength grew. The places I was overlooked are now the places where I'm being seen and sent.

I want to say this clearly for anyone reading—especially the one who thinks your story has been too messy for God to use: You're exactly the one He came for.

You don't have to understand the road.

You just have to keep walking it with Him.

Because every mile matters.

Every tear is counted.

Every closed door is preparation for something better.

And nothing—not even the ugliest chapters—are wasted when He's the author.

King James Version (KJV):
"And we know that all things work together for good
to them that love God,
to them who are the called according to his purpose."
Romans 8:28 (KJV)

Chapter Fifteen:

"When Everything Changes"

I used to think breakthroughs came in lightning strikes—loud, undeniable, sudden. But sometimes, it shows up in the quiet. In a whisper. In a changed heart. In a prayer that finally got answered after years of silence.

The year my daughter had brain surgery was the year everything changed.

Not just for her, but for us all.

Some stories don't start with a bang — they begin in a hospital room, quiet and sterile, where everything you've ever believed gets put to the test. Mine began with a diagnosis that could have broken me. But it didn't. Because God was already in the room.

"Ependymoma." The doctor said it so matter-of-factly. A malignant tumor. Chemo and radiation needed immediately. My daughter's life hanging in the balance. But something in my spirit wouldn't settle. I didn't have medical degrees or influence — I barely had her. Trusting others to make all the choices for her medical care.

Her grandmother and I had never been close. We weren't even on speaking terms most of the time. But that diagnosis brought us to the same table. For once, we weren't pulling against each other. We were fighting for the same little girl. And somehow, that cracked the ice.

We got a second opinion. Then a third. And what they found was not cancer—it was benign. A completely different diagnosis. No chemo. No radiation. Just surgery. Just healing.

God had walked into that hospital room before we ever did.

I didn't have control, but I had faith.

I didn't have support from everyone, but I had favor.

I didn't have a title or a home address or a picture-perfect past, but I had a seat in that room because I was her mother.

And heaven backed me.

In Charlotte, I was treated with dignity. The doctors included me. God moved us out of my hometown—out of the shadows of my past—and into a new place, where I wasn't "that girl" from before. I was just a mom, praying for her child.

I slept in my car outside the hospital some nights. I rotated between family members' homes. I cried. I wrote songs. I journaled. I stayed. Because that's what love does.

That season taught me that God's timing is surgical. Precise. Perfect. And His plans aren't made to fit our comfort—they're made to show His glory.

Her healing wasn't just physical. It healed me too.

It healed family dynamics.

It healed old wounds.

It awakened dreams I didn't know were still breathing.

I still remember hearing God say, "She's my child. I've just loaned her to you."

That moment shattered every illusion of control I had.

It was the moment I truly let go.

King James Version (KJV):
"For I know the thoughts that I think toward you, saith the Lord, thoughts of peace, and not of evil,
to give you an expected end."
Jeremiah 29:11 (KJV)

Chapter Sixteen:

"No One But God"

There were days I wanted to give up. Days where the weight of the race crushed my chest, where my knees hit the ground from exhaustion—not out of prayer, but pain. My kid was 18. She was grown. The system said she no longer needed me. The courts had made their decisions. The doctors had made theirs. And life? Life didn't wait for me to catch my breath.

I remember thinking: What's the point now?

But the truth is—God wasn't done.

Every sacrifice, every sleepless night, every tear screamed into a steering wheel, it meant something. I didn't run the race for a certificate or an applause. I ran it for love. I ran it because somewhere deep in my gut I knew God had called me to something greater. Something I couldn't see just yet.

Even when I lost hope in the journey, God kept breathing into my lungs.

That's what Chapter 16 became—the chapter where I let go of what should've happened and leaned into what could still be. The one where I found out the race wasn't over. I wasn't running aimlessly—I was running toward purpose.

And purpose doesn't expire when your child turns 18.

No.

Purpose starts when you realize the pain didn't kill you.

And if it didn't kill you—God's going to use it.

<blockquote>
King James Version (KJV):
"Being confident of this very thing,
that he which hath begun a good work in you
will perform it until the day of Jesus Christ."
Philippians 1:6 (KJV)
</blockquote>

Chapter Seventeen:

"The Turning Point"

There comes a moment in every long journey when you stop looking at the mountain and start realizing—you're already halfway up. That was this chapter for me. I had cried the tears. I had driven the miles. I had fought invisible battles no one saw but God. And somehow—I was still standing.

Something changed in me. Maybe it was the silence that followed all the noise. Or the realization that even though I didn't have the ending I pictured, I was living a story still being written. My daughter was alive. I was alive. And we were both still becoming.

This chapter was less about proving something and more about accepting what had already been proven. God's grace was not only enough—it was everything. I had fought so hard to become stable, to become seen, to be heard. But now, I was learning to be still. To stop striving and start trusting. To stop surviving and start living.

I didn't have to be famous. I didn't need everyone to understand. I just needed to obey.

I had seen miracles. I had survived heartbreaks. And I had made it to a place where I could say:

"This is not the end. This is the turning point."

King James Version (KJV):
"And let us not be weary in doing good:
for in due season we shall reap,
if we faint not."
Galatians 6:9 (KJV)

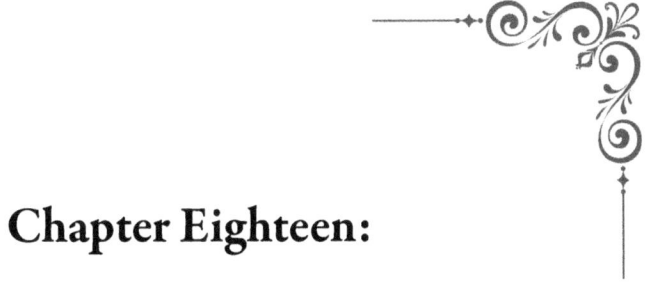

Chapter Eighteen:

"When the Weight Hits You Back"

After the turning point, you expect the weight to lift—but sometimes, it hits harder. Not because you're weaker, but because you've finally stopped running. And once you stop running, you can feel everything.

That's what happened to me. After all the fighting, after all the declarations of faith, after all the small victories—I felt tired. Not sleepy tired. Soul tired. The kind of tired that makes you ask, "God... what now?"

My daughter had turned 18. My biggest goals had been reached: she was alive, and I had created a stable life. But instead of celebrating, I felt like I was falling apart. I had given everything. And I mean everything. There were days I didn't know if I could do another prayer, another hope, another mile.

The mountain was climbed. But I still didn't feel like I had arrived.

But that's when God whispered to me, "You weren't climbing to a destination... you were climbing to become."

That revelation began to break something open in me. I realized that the journey is the blessing. The weight I was carrying wasn't punishment—it was evidence. Evidence that I had not given up. That I was still running with purpose. That I was still willing to believe when belief felt fragile.

I didn't want to give up... but I did need to pause. Not to quit. But to breathe. To exhale everything I was trying to hold together, and remember who was really holding me.

God had brought me this far.

And He wasn't about to leave me here.

King James Version (KJV):
"Come unto me, all ye that labour and are heavy laden,
and I will give you rest."

Matthew 11:28 (KJV)

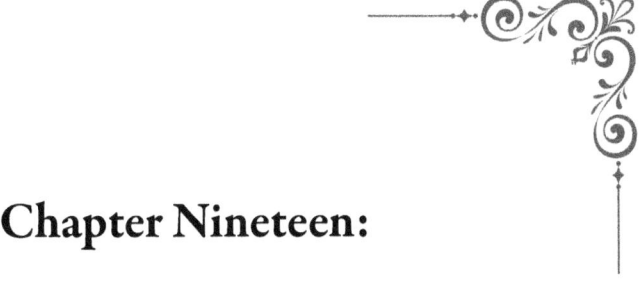

Chapter Nineteen:

"Rest, Reset, Rise"

The race had left me breathless. Not because I lost, but because I ran so hard, so long, and so alone. But this chapter wasn't about pushing through — it was about laying it all down.

I realized I didn't need to prove anything anymore. I had already done the impossible. I had carried my child through brain surgery. I had fought for over a decade to reclaim my motherhood. I had survived abuse, addiction, homelessness, rejection, shame, and silence. And I was still here. Still standing. Still sane. Still saved.

This chapter of my life felt different. There was no loud applause. No spotlight. Just stillness. A quiet place where God began to reintroduce me to myself.

He reminded me that rest isn't weakness — it's worship.

Resetting doesn't mean quitting — it means realigning.

And rising? Well, that's just what happens naturally when you've been in the valley long enough.

I started to look in the mirror and see a woman I didn't recognize...

not because she was lost, but because she was new. God had rebuilt me from the inside out. The things that used to break me didn't anymore.

The people who used to shake me had no power anymore. I no longer needed validation to believe I was valuable. I knew it. And that changed everything.

King James Version (KJV):
"But they that wait upon the Lord shall renew their strength;
they shall mount up with wings as eagles;
they shall run, and not be weary;
and they shall walk, and not faint."
Isaiah 40:31 (KJV)

Chapter Twenty:

"Pressing Forward with Fire"

I had caught my breath — and now, I was coming with fire.

Something shifted in me after the stillness. The ache didn't disappear, but it transformed. What used to weigh me down now became fuel. It was as if everything I had endured had been thrown into a furnace, and instead of burning me out, it refined me.

I didn't feel like a victim anymore. I felt like a vessel — one that had been crushed but not destroyed, poured out but never empty. The world had told me "you're too late," "you're too broken," "you'll never make it back," but I knew better now. I had proof that God rewrites stories. I was the proof.

There was a boldness rising in me that I hadn't known before. A holy urgency. I started waking up with purpose again. Not chasing people. Not chasing approval. Just chasing Him.

I knew there was more to do, and this time, I wasn't doing it to be seen — I was doing it because I was called. The truth is, people might never understand the depth of what God brought me through. They might not even believe it. But they'll see the fruit. Because I'm not just telling a story anymore — I am the story.

God has handed me the pen again.

And this time, I'm writing with fire.

King James Version (KJV):
"I press toward the mark for the prize of the high calling of God in Christ Jesus."
Philippians 3:14 (KJV)

Chapter Twenty-One:

"A Legacy in the Making"

This wasn't just about healing anymore — this was about building. Once, all I could think about was surviving the storm. Now, I could see something even more powerful: legacy. What good is healing if you don't use it to help others rise? What's the point of walking through the fire if you don't come out with a torch to light the way for someone else?

God didn't bring me this far to keep quiet. He brought me through the mud and fire so I could speak, create, write, and leave something behind — something my daughter could stand on, something generations would feel.

I started dreaming again, but not just for me. I dreamed of building something so beautiful, so rooted in truth, that it would outlive me. Books, songs, businesses, ministries, spaces of peace, creativity, and belonging. Things that spoke of God's goodness long after my voice was gone.

For years, my goals were survival.

Now they are eternal.

I may not have millions in the bank, but I am rich in experience, favor, mercy, and the fingerprints of God on my life. And every time I look back, I'm reminded — the same God that carried me this far will complete the work He started. It's not on me to make it all happen. It's on me to move when He says move, speak when He says speak, and trust Him with the outcome.

This chapter is about legacy — not just the kind the world can measure, but the kind heaven keeps a record of.

King James Version (KJV):
"Being confident of this very thing,
that he who hath begun a good work in you
will perform it until the day of Jesus Christ."

Philippians 1:6 (KJV)

Chapter Twenty-Two:

"When You've Seen Too Much to Go Back"

By now, I've walked through too many valleys with God to ever doubt His presence again.

I'VE BEEN IN ROOMS where my voice didn't matter.
I've stood beside hospital beds where the outcome was uncertain.
I've handed over my daughter to surgeries I couldn't stop.
I've slept in cars, hidden in shadows, cried behind closed doors —
but I've also witnessed miracles.
I've felt angels brush past me in the middle of prayer.
I've seen provision fall out of nowhere, like manna in the wilderness.
And when I couldn't stand, God stood for me.
So now? Even when things get hard — I can't go back.

There's no version of me that can live like I used to. There's no comfort in the old pain. That season of my life is closed, even if I still feel the wind of it sometimes. The pain taught me obedience. The hunger taught me to pray. The losses taught me how to see.

And most importantly — *the suffering taught me how to listen.*
I don't need a pulpit to know I've been called.
I don't need applause to believe that my life carries power.
I know what I carry now, and I know who carries me.

There is something holy about getting to the other side of grief and still choosing joy.

Something sacred about surviving the fire and refusing to smell like smoke.

I no longer chase approval — I chase purpose.

And that, right there, is the difference between someone who's still searching and someone who's been found.

King James Version (KJV):
"But none of these things move me,
neither count I my life dear unto myself,
so that I might finish my course with joy."
Acts 20:24 (KJV)

Chapter Twenty-Three:

"The Kind of Strength That Can't Be Faked"

There's a strength that comes from being broken in ways no one can see.
A strength that doesn't shout — it stands. Quietly.
Even when the knees are trembling.
This chapter is about that strength.
It's the kind that lets you keep showing up when there's no applause, no paycheck, and no guarantee that what you're doing will even work. It's the kind that grows in silence. It grows in rooms where no one says "I'm proud of you." It grows in the tears cried at red lights, in the prayers whispered into steering wheels, in the nights you stay up writing because you refuse to let your story die.

I don't fake being strong anymore. I am strong. Because I've had to be.
Not for attention. Not for clout. But for legacy.
I had a little girl to fight for — and now I've got a whole vision to birth. I'm still figuring it all out, but I'm doing it with courage. And that courage? It was hard-earned. It came from betrayal, disappointment, heartbreak, and survival.
But it's real.
And maybe that's the most powerful thing I can offer the world — the realest version of me.
A woman who got back up.
A mother who never quit.
A daughter of God who still believes in miracles, even with the scars.
Because the truth is: nothing in this world can stop someone who's been rebuilt by grace.

King James Version (KJV):
"My grace is sufficient for thee:

for my strength is made perfect in weakness."
2 Corinthians 12:9 (KJV)

Chapter Twenty-Four:

"Running on Grace, Not Fumes"

I used to run on empty — emotionally, spiritually, physically.
I thought if I just pushed harder, prayed longer, stayed busy, I could outrun the ache.
But the truth is, running on fumes isn't noble — it's dangerous.
It's God's grace I need, not my grit.
In this chapter, I stopped idolizing hustle and started asking God for help. Real help.
Not just to "make it through," but to thrive.

I started paying attention to the ways I was burning myself out trying to prove I was worthy. To prove I was enough. I learned that worthiness isn't earned — it's inherited. I'm my Father's daughter. I don't have to strive for what's already mine.

And even now, when exhaustion creeps in or fear starts to whisper, I remember:

I'm not running this race to impress anyone.
I'm running it because there's a legacy attached to my name.
There's a little girl who watches me.
There's a God who calls me.
There's a story that can heal people.
So I slowed down.
I started listening.
To my body.
To the Spirit.
To the truth.
And the truth is: I'm not running alone.

I never was.

King James Version (KJV):
"But they that wait upon the Lord shall renew their strength;
they shall mount up with wings as eagles;
they shall run, and not be weary;
and they shall walk, and not faint."
Isaiah 40:31 (KJV)

Chapter Twenty-Five:

"The Reward of Returning"

There's a certain kind of beauty in returning —
 not just physically, but spiritually.
I've learned that the return is often more powerful than the run.
And for me, coming back wasn't about returning to people, places, or even goals...
 it was about returning to God.
 To truth.
 To myself.
 I used to think once something was lost, it was over.
 If I lost time, I thought I'd never get it back.
 If I lost relationships, I thought they were gone for good.
 But God doesn't work like we do.
 He's the God of restoration.
 The Redeemer of time.
 The Healer of hearts.
 This chapter of my life — this season — has been a gentle reminder
 that what's broken can be rebuilt,
 what's delayed can still be delivered,
 and what's dead can be resurrected.
 Returning didn't look like I thought it would.
 It looked like sleeping in my car and still praising.
 It looked like hearing my daughter say "I love you" again after brain surgery.
 It looked like getting up, again and again,
 even when my body and heart said "stay down."
 But I made it.

Not perfect, not polished, but present.
And that's enough.

God is in the business of bringing us back.
And when He does, He doesn't scold us.
He celebrates us.

King James Version (KJV):
"So I will restore to you the years that the swarming locust has eaten..."
Joel 2:25 (KJV)

Chapter Twenty-Six:

"Favor in the Fire"

There's something you learn when you walk through flames and come out without the smell of smoke.

It's not just survival—it's transformation.

It's seeing firsthand that God doesn't always put out the fire.

Sometimes He gets in it with you.

Like Shadrach, Meshach, and Abednego, I found that the fire didn't consume me—it refined me.

I've been in rooms where I felt invisible.

I've stood in places where my name was dismissed before I ever had a chance to speak.

I've been misunderstood, mislabeled, and underestimated.

And yet... I kept showing up.

Not because I felt the need to prove anything,

but because I knew God was still writing my story.

He was still teaching me how to recognize His voice—

confirming that it was Him who gave the vision,

the dream,

the direction,

and the wisdom to steward every resource well

and not waste what He provides.

Don't beat yourself up over what was at stake —

the Lord says nothing stolen will be lacking.

His supply doesn't run dry.

He is ever-present, sovereign, and full of justice.

He can move anywhere, at any time, in any way He chooses.

He is brilliant, powerful, and faithful.
You don't have to protect yourself — He already is.
Trust what He has planned for you—because it's not ordinary, it's extraordinary.
God doesn't do average; He exceeds expectations,
going beyond anything we could ever ask, think, or imagine.
No matter where you are in life, know this —
if you keep drawing closer to Him,
He won't leave a single thread unfinished.
I know it doesn't always feel that way,
but I'm living proof that Jesus Christ can take what seems like nothing
and transform it into something more beautiful than you've ever imagined—
something I had never seen before in my own life.
His spiritual gifts are precise, intentional,
and serve as confirmation that our names are written in the Lamb's Book of Life.
These gifts are just a glimpse of His goodness—
He Himself is the greatest gift of all.
Pursue Jesus, seek His righteousness,
and everything else will follow.
His favor is what carried me when I didn't even know how to walk.
His favor is what made doors open that no résumé could justify.
His favor gave me moments that no man could orchestrate—
like sitting in a hospital room, unwanted and unwelcome, yet full of peace.

***The kind of peace that doesn't make sense
unless you've met the Prince of it.***

There's no mistaking it:
I didn't get here by luck.
I didn't survive by coincidence.
I was carried by grace.
I was covered by mercy.
I was chosen—even in the chaos.
Favor doesn't always look like riches.
Sometimes it looks like resilience.
Sometimes it looks like surviving abuse, addiction, and abandonment.
Sometimes it looks like standing on stages you only dreamed of—
while knowing your real reward was built in silence, in suffering, in secret.

King James Version (KJV):
"When you walk through the fire, you shall not be burned,
nor shall the flame scorch you."
Isaiah 43:2 (KJV)

*Trust in all He's written
with His hand divine
It won't be simple, common, or confined.
For He moves in wonder,
paints with light,
Exceeds your dreams
in day and night.
What He prepares,
the heart can't see.
It's more than hope,
it's destiny.*

Chapter Twenty-Seven:

"The Roots Beneath the Rise"

Everyone sees the flower when it blooms,
   but no one really talks about the soil—
the dirt, the darkness, the pressure beneath the surface that made it grow.
People clap when the light hits you right,
but they didn't see the nights you cried alone in your car,
hoping the sun would come up and somehow bring clarity.
They didn't hear the silent prayers whispered in rest-stop parking lots
or feel the ache of seeing your child from a distance,
knowing you've done all you can—
and it still hasn't been enough to bring them home.
But God saw.
God heard.
And God knew.
This season has been about going deeper than I ever wanted to.
Learning to trust God in the unseen.
Realizing that even though the fruit took time to show,
the roots were being strengthened the whole time.
This chapter of my life isn't about everything looking perfect—
it's about being grounded.
About building something real.
No longer moved by what people say or how they misunderstand my story.
No longer shaken when love doesn't show up the way I hoped.
I've anchored myself in something more solid than emotion: truth.
And the truth is, I didn't make it this far to fold.
I didn't suffer for nothing.

I didn't fight for this life, just to hand it over to fear.
God has been rebuilding me.
Not on shaky ground, but on rock.
On wisdom.
On lessons learned the hard way.
And I'm okay with that.
Because I'm not here to impress.
I'm here to grow.
To heal.
To rise.
To teach my daughter what it means to endure.
And maybe, just maybe,
she'll know that God can take broken things and make them whole.
That roots matter more than petals.
That beauty built in pain... lasts.

King James Version (KJV):
"Being confident of this very thing,
that He which hath begun a good work in you
will perform it until the day of Jesus Christ."
Philippians 1:6 (KJV)

Chapter Twenty-Eight:

"The Battle for Worth"

It's not just the world you fight—
sometimes it's your own mind.
The battle doesn't always look like swords and shields.
Sometimes it looks like shame, silence, and memories that try to define you.
I've walked through valleys where I questioned everything:
Am I enough?
Will I ever be stable enough, healed enough, good enough?
Why is my child still waiting to come home to me?
These thoughts come like waves, and they don't ask for permission.
But I've learned—
I don't have to believe every thought that knocks.
I've come to know the voice of God more intimately than I've known the voices of my past.
He doesn't shame.
He doesn't condemn.
He speaks life, and when He speaks, it quiets every other noise.
Yes, I've made mistakes.
Yes, I've walked through fire.
But my worth was never tied to my perfection—
it was always rooted in my redemption.
When people look at me, they might see what they think I've done
or who they think I am,
but they didn't see the moments when I chose God over comfort.
They weren't there when I gave up what I wanted most
in order to protect my daughter.

Or when I stayed quiet in rooms where I had every right to defend myself,
but I chose peace.
God has taught me that value isn't in what others can see—
it's in what He planted in me.
And when God plants something, it doesn't matter how long it takes to bloom—
it will.
This chapter of my life isn't just about survival anymore—
it's about standing in confidence.
Not arrogance.
Not pride.
But holy boldness.
Because when you know who you are,
you don't have to prove it.
And when you've been through what I've been through,
peace becomes your greatest flex.

>King James Version (KJV):
>"The Lord will fight for you,
>and you shall hold your peace."
>Exodus 14:14 (KJV)

Chapter Twenty-Nine:

"Peace Turned Power"

There comes a moment when peace isn't just stillness—
it becomes strategy.
A holy kind of power.
A divine exchange.
Not loud. Not showy.
Just steady.
Like a river beneath the surface, carving stone over time.
That's what God has been doing in me.
I used to crave stability because everything felt so unstable.
But now, I crave obedience.
Because obedience is what leads to peace,
and peace is the seed of power.
Not the kind of power that controls others—
but the kind that keeps you grounded when the storm comes again.
I remember when I used to equate silence with weakness.
When I thought saying nothing meant I was being walked over.
Now I see, silence has saved me more than speaking ever has.
God's whisper has redirected my entire life.
And I've learned—
the strongest woman in the room is often the one who doesn't need to prove it.
I've seen God turn my sleepless nights into songs.
I've seen Him breathe life into words I didn't even think anyone would read.
I've seen Him soften hearts that once felt stone cold toward me—

including my own.
Peace taught me patience.
But power taught me to move.
To take steps without full clarity.
To walk by faith when sight failed.
To believe for healing before I ever saw progress.
To pour out love when all I wanted was to be held.
God has shown me that He doesn't waste anything—
not the pain,
not the past,
not even the pauses.
This is what power looks like:

- It's choosing to believe that your prayers are doing more than your panic ever could.
- It's walking into places that once broke you, and holding your head high because you know Who walks with you.
- It's raising your daughter from a place of joy instead of guilt.
- It's being okay with slow progress, as long as it's God's pace.

Power isn't just in doing more.
It's in knowing you don't have to do it alone.
     King James Version (KJV):
     "But he said to me,
    My grace is sufficient for thee:
 for my strength is made perfect in weakness."
     2 Corinthians 12:9 (KJV)

Chapter Thirty:

"The Calling with Both Hands Open"

There's something sacred about finally saying yes with your whole heart.
No backup plan.
No hesitation.
Just—yes, Lord.
I used to grip everything so tightly.
Dreams.
People.
Outcomes.
I was scared that if I didn't hold on, it would all slip away.
But God wasn't asking me to hold tighter—He was asking me to release it.
To stop calling survival "obedience"
and start walking in real surrender.
This chapter of my life didn't come with confetti.
It came with clarity.
And a decision.
I'm not running after what the world told me I needed.
I'm not chasing applause or positions or people who never saw me.
I'm chasing what He whispered in the quiet.
And I'm doing it with both hands open.
Open hands mean no manipulation.
Open hands mean no begging.
Open hands mean trust.

MY CALLING WAS NEVER just about me—

it was about legacy.
About redemption.
About reaching my daughter with truth when lies once surrounded her.
It's about building a life I don't have to escape from.
A home that feels like heaven.
A voice that speaks to more than just pain—
it speaks to purpose.
And yes, I still doubt sometimes.
I still hear the voice that says "you're too late" or "too damaged."
But now I know better.
Because God doesn't call the qualified.
He qualifies the called.
And I've been called.
Not just to create—but to conquer.
To speak what I once whispered.
To help others fly when they've only ever crawled.
To pull people from the pit and point them to the One who lifted me out.
I can't say I know every step from here,
but I know the next one.
And I'll take it—
open handed.

Open hearted.
All in.

> King James Version (KJV):
> "And the Lord answered me, and said,
> Write the vision, and make it plain upon tables,
> that he may run that readeth it."
> Habakkuk 2:2 (KJV)

Chapter Thirty-One:

"The Sound of Purpose"

There's a sound purpose makes when it finally breaks through.
It's not always a trumpet or a shout—
sometimes, it's a whisper that silences the lies.
Sometimes, it's the soft click of a locked door finally opening after years of knocking.
For me, the sound of purpose was music—
not just in melody, but in meaning.
It was every tear that hit the dashboard.
Every whispered prayer.
Every "God, I don't know what to do, but I trust You anyway."
There was a moment I will never forget.
I sat in silence after a long day of working, serving, praying,
and still feeling unseen.
I was exhausted.
Tired from the spiritual warfare.
Tired of waiting.
Tired of hoping for healing.
And in that silence, a melody rose up in my spirit.
No instruments.
No audience.
Just God and me.
And He said:
"You don't have to try to be enough. You already are."
In that moment, I wept—
not because I was broken,

but because something in me healed.
Purpose had always been chasing me.
It just had to wait until I stopped running.
Purpose isn't a place,
it's a presence.
It's what happens when your life stops echoing the voices of your past
and starts resonating with the voice of your Father.
Everything started sounding different.
- My "no" had power.
- My "yes" had intention.
- My silence became sacred.
- My words carried weight.

Now, I create from overflow, not desperation.
I no longer hustle for worth—
I walk in it.
And my child?
She hears the music too.
Even through her healing journey,
she recognizes the rhythm of resilience.
This chapter is about reclaiming what I thought was lost.
About dancing again—
not for dollars, but for destiny.
Singing again—
not to be heard, but to glorify the One who never stopped listening.
Writing again—
not because I'm empty, but because He filled me.
The sound of purpose is steady now.
Like footsteps on holy ground.

> King James Version (KJV):
> "For we are his workmanship,
> created in Christ Jesus unto good works,
> which God hath before ordained that we should walk in them."
> Ephesians 2:10 (KJV)

Chapter Thirty-Two:

"Destiny Wasn't Delayed, It Was Developed"

Sometimes, the things we think are holding us back are actually holding us together.

I used to look at every detour, every delay, every door slammed in my face and wonder if I had missed it.

Maybe I wasn't worthy.

Maybe I had waited too long.

Maybe too much damage had been done.

But then God whispered, "I was building you in the waiting."

This chapter isn't about being stuck—

it's about being strengthened.

It's about realizing that the wilderness didn't waste time,

it prepared me for the weight of glory that's coming.

You see, destiny doesn't rush.

It refines.

It chisels.

It humbles.

It rewrites the parts of your story you thought were too messy to matter.

All this time, I thought I was being overlooked.

But I wasn't overlooked—

I was being overhauled.

God was developing me in secret so He could trust me in the spotlight.

Not just with gifts, but with grace.

Not just with success, but with stewardship.

Not just with influence, but with integrity.

I had to learn how to be content in hidden places.

- Content when no one clapped.
- Content when no one called.
- Content when I was just learning how to breathe again.

Destiny doesn't come to those who demand it.

It comes to those who are devoted when no one's watching.

And now I see—

I wasn't behind schedule.

I was being developed for something greater.

So no, I wasn't delayed.

I wasn't denied.

I was being designed by the Master Himself.

Now, I can walk into rooms I used to cry outside of.

Now, I can speak with authority because I lived through what others only imagined.

Now, I can show my daughter what God can do with someone who refuses to give up.

Destiny didn't skip me.

It was waiting for me to grow into it.

> King James Version (KJV):
> "But let patience have her perfect work,
> that ye may be perfect and entire, wanting nothing."
> James 1:4 (KJV)

Chapter Thirty-Three:

"The Door Only God Could Open"

You know those moments when everything shifts?
Not just a little—
but the kind of shift that lets you know Heaven moved.
Chapter 33 is about that kind of moment.
All my life, I had been trying to open doors.
Kicking, pulling, twisting knobs that weren't mine to touch.
Hustling in my own strength, trying to earn what only God could give by grace.
But then came the door—
the one I didn't force.
It swung open so smoothly I almost missed the miracle in its motion.
No resistance.
No manipulation.
No striving.
And that's when I knew...
This wasn't my doing.
It was His.
I wasn't qualified by the world's standards.
I didn't have the degree.
I didn't have the connections.
I didn't even have a steady place to sleep.

BUT I DID HAVE FAVOR.
And when you have favor—

that's enough.
That open door didn't just bless me,
it confirmed something I desperately needed to hear:
"You are not forgotten. I have plans for you. I trust you with more now."
Maybe someone reading this needs to hear it too.

THAT THING YOU THOUGHT you missed?
If it was for you, it's coming back around.
That opportunity you think you're too late for?
God can resurrect timelines.
When God opens a door, no man can shut it.
Not your past.
Not your failures.
Not even your self-doubt.
This was the beginning of something new.
And unlike before—
I was ready.
Not perfect, but prepared.
Not confident in myself, but fully convinced in Him.
The kind of door that leads to your real purpose isn't flashy—
it's faithful.
It shows up right when you're about to give up.
And when it does, you'll walk through it and whisper, "Only God."

BECAUSE DEEP DOWN, you'll know
you weren't strong enough to pull this off...
...but you were surrendered enough to receive it.
King James Version (KJV):
"I have set before thee an open door,
and no man can shut it."
Revelation 3:8 (KJV)

Chapter Thirty-Four:

"I'm Not Going Back"

You ever look at your life and realize—
there's nothing back there for me?
Not the old habits.
Not the old people.
Not even the old mindset.
There was a time I wrestled with going back.
Not because it was good, but because it was familiar.
Back then, I knew how to survive.
I knew what to expect.
Even if it hurt, I could predict the pain.
But God started breaking that cycle.
And once you taste peace, clarity, and purpose—
you lose the appetite for confusion, chaos, and crumbs.
I don't care how glittery it looks...
if it doesn't bring me closer to Him, I can't go back.
There were moments I wanted to.
Nights sleeping in my car.
Days when silence echoed louder than encouragement.
I questioned,
"What if I never get there? What if I'm too late?"
But then I remembered—
I've already come too far.

GOING BACK MEANT DENYING all the progress God made in me.

Going back meant rejecting every answered prayer.
Going back meant putting back on the chains I cried for Him to break.
Nah.
Not me.
I'm not going back.
That means no going back to people who only loved the broken version of me.
No going back to jobs that drained me.
No going back to the girl who doubted her worth.
That version of me is buried.
And resurrection only comes through Christ—not cycles.
I'm not returning to survival mode when God promised abundant life.
I'm not rehearsing the trauma He already healed.
And I'm not dumbing down my testimony to make people comfortable.
He didn't bring me through that
just to turn around and go back to this.
So if you see me walking different, talking bolder, dreaming louder...
It's because I've seen what's behind me—
and I've finally decided...

I'm not going back...
Neither are you.

>King James Version (KJV):
>"But Jesus said unto him,
>No man, having put his hand to the plow, and looking back,
>is fit for the kingdom of God."
>Luke 9:62 (KJV)

Chapter Thirty-Five:

"What I'm Fighting For"

It's more than just surviving.
It's more than just a bed, a job, or a title.
This is warfare for legacy.
I've fought through pain that wanted to paralyze me.
I've pushed through sleepless nights and bitter mornings
just to prove to myself—
and to my daughter—
that we are not what we've been through.
I'm fighting for her to know what it means to be safe.
To feel seen.
To be free to be exactly who God created her to be, without apology.
This isn't about proving anything to the people who said I wouldn't make it.
This isn't about proving I can bounce back from failure.
It's about proving to myself that I am capable of healing,
of growing,
of becoming everything God whispered to me in the dark.
I'm fighting for the child in me who was told to be quiet.
For the teenage girl who thought she had to give her body to feel loved.
For the woman who almost gave up
when she lost her child and her mind at the same time.

I'M FIGHTING FOR GENERATIONAL change.
For curses to be broken.

For joy to become normal, not a rare occurrence.
I'm fighting for a home where peace lives.
Where laughter doesn't have to be earned.
Where God's presence isn't a Sunday visit but an everyday encounter.
I'm fighting to stay in purpose, even when the path is unfamiliar.
Because if I give up now, I forfeit everything I've prayed for.
This fight is spiritual.
It's personal.
It's holy.
And I've decided—
I may get tired,
but I'm not backing down.
Every time I've wanted to quit,
God reminded me why I started.

> *I'm not fighting for fame.*
> *I'm not fighting for followers.*
> *I'm fighting for a future.*

One my daughter can stand in
without needing to heal from what I didn't face.

> King James Version (KJV):
> "Fight the good fight of faith,
> lay hold on eternal life,
> whereunto thou art also called…"
> 1 Timothy 6:12 (KJV)

Chapter Thirty-Six:

"When It Finally Starts Making Sense"

It didn't make sense when I was crying alone in the car.
It didn't make sense when I gave my last dollar to see my kid smile for five minutes.

It didn't make sense when people assumed the worst while I was giving it my best.

But now—

It's starting to.

When I look at the pain, the decisions, the near-death moments,

and even the guilt I carried like a weighted coat—

I see how God weaved it into something only He could.

I used to ask, "Why me?"

Now I ask,

"Who else but me could have survived this and still love like I do?"

The lessons didn't come through comfort.

They came through chaos.

They came when I lost what I thought I needed

to discover what I truly had.

I thought I needed approval.

I needed peace.

I thought I needed a partner.

I needed purpose.

I thought I needed more time.

I needed more trust in the One who already saw the end from the beginning.

THE PIECES STARTED clicking into place
when I stopped trying to control the picture.
I was looking for validation when God was offering me vision.
My daughter still asks to live with me.
And I still want to say yes every time.
But the wisdom I've gained says,
"Not yet—not until the foundation is solid."
I'm building her something permanent.
All of the stories, the near misses, the times I nearly gave up—
it's all a part of it.
And now, instead of shame, I feel strategy.
Instead of loss, I see launch points.
Instead of failure, I see faithfulness—
His, not mine.
Because if this were up to me,
I wouldn't have made it.
But since it's up to God,
nothing is wasted.
This chapter is proof.
This book is proof.
I am proof.

King James Version (KJV):
"And we know that all things work together for good
to them that love God,
to them who are the called according to his purpose."
Romans 8:28 (KJV)

Chapter Thirty-Seven:

"The Wait Wasn't Wasted"

It wasn't just a delay—
    it was development.
It wasn't just silence—
it was stretching.
It wasn't just a no—
it was not yet, because something better was being built.
I used to think the wait was punishment.
Now I see it was protection.
I didn't know then what I know now:
God holds time, and He never rushes glory.
In the quiet places, I grew.
In the hidden places, I healed.
In the seasons where I was overlooked,
I was actually being preserved.
Had the doors opened too soon,
I might've let the wrong people in.
Had I received the blessings early,
I might've lost them to insecurity, fear, or the need to prove something.
But now?
Now I can carry them with character.
There were nights I didn't want to wake up.
There were mornings I didn't want to rise.

AND YET...

Here I am.
Still breathing.
Still writing.
Still believing.
God was not just making a way for me.
He was making a way through me.
I thought I was stuck—
but I was being sent.
I thought I was behind—
but I was being refined.
The wait taught me how to pray.
How to stand.
How to speak the Word like it was the very oxygen I needed to survive.
Because some days—
it was.

SO IF YOU'RE STILL waiting, let me remind you:
    The wait is holy ground.
    It's not dead time.
    It's seed time.
    And baby,
    the harvest is coming.

King James Version (KJV):
"But they that wait upon the LORD shall renew their strength;
they shall mount up with wings as eagles;
they shall run, and not be weary;
and they shall walk, and not faint."
Isaiah 40:31 (KJV)

Chapter Thirty-Eight:

"Where I'm Headed Is Not Where I Started"

If you only knew where I came from...
The nights I cried silently,
the mornings I woke up numb.
The days I had no gas, no hope, no plan—
just God.
And that was enough.
I started this journey broken, ashamed, uncertain.
I questioned my worth, doubted my purpose,
and tried to disappear more than once.
But here's what I know now:
God doesn't need a perfect beginning.
He just needs a willing heart.
I was never supposed to stay in survival mode.
He called me to build, to blossom, to be bold.
The trauma I carried tried to tell me who I was.
But the truth of God redefined me—
not by my past, not by my pain—
but by His plans.
I've learned to stop giving explanations
to people who never cared to understand.

This season is personal.
This victory is personal.
This calling—it's mine.
I'm not waiting for applause.
I'm not waiting for permission.
I'm not chasing validation.
I'm after impact.
Where I'm headed is somewhere the old me wouldn't have recognized.
Because the old me was just trying to survive.
But the woman I am now?
She's learning how to soar.
I'm no longer afraid to say,
"I deserve joy."
I deserve peace.
I deserve to be loved right.
Not because of what I've done—
but because of what He's done in me.
The wilderness didn't destroy me.
It taught me to hear Him clearly.
I used to beg God to change my situation.
Now I thank Him that He changed me first.
This isn't the end.
This is the rise.
This is the moment the shift becomes visible.

LET THEM LOOK CONFUSED.
Let them ask questions.
Let them think or assume.
Don't be distracted like Nehemiah on the wall.
Dogs don't bark at parked cars.
No one tries to hit someone who isn't carrying the ball.

The devil only comes after what is a threat to him and he will do anything to distort the image of God in any way he can.
NOW REMEMBER THAT!

LET THEM THINK IT'S sudden.
    But you and I know—
    it was always coming.
    This is just the *beginning of the unfolding.*
                    King James Version (KJV):
"Remember not the former things, neither consider the things of old.
    Behold, I will do a new thing; now it shall spring forth;
            shall ye not know it?"
              Isaiah 43:18–19 (KJV)

Chapter Thirty-Nine:

"The Gift of Clear Vision"

There was a time I couldn't see.
 Not just physically, but spiritually, emotionally... directionally.
I was walking in the dark—
reacting to life instead of moving with purpose.
But then...
God touched my eyes.
Not in the way you'd expect.
Not with fireworks or thunder.
But in the quiet places,
in the stillness between heartbreak and hope,
He whispered, "Look again."
Look again at who you are.
Look again at what you've survived.
Look again at what I've placed in your hands.
I used to confuse movement with progress.
But now I know—vision is more powerful than speed.
When God shows you where you're going,
you don't have to rush.
You can walk with bold, beautiful clarity.
The distractions still come.
But I don't chase every opportunity, every opinion, or every door.
Now I ask:

IS IT ALIGNED? IS IT God? Or is it noise?

Because I've lived long enough in confusion.
I've paid the price for unclear boundaries,
blurred relationships,
and foggy faith.
That's over now.
This is the season of clear vision.
I see it now.
I see the ministry, the message, the mission.
I see the legacy, not just the lack.
I see my daughter, not just her diagnosis.
I see the power in my pen,
the healing in my story,
and the authority in my voice.
The same God who gave sight to the blind,
is giving me new vision every day.
I'm not guessing anymore.
I'm guided.
And now,
I don't just see with my eyes—
I see with my spirit.

>King James Version (KJV):
>"Where there is no vision, the people perish:
>but he that keepeth the law, happy is he."
>Proverbs 29:18 (KJV)

Chapter Forty:

"From Barefoot to Bold"

I remember when my feet were bare—
    not just literally, but spiritually.
I was exposed.
Vulnerable.
Unprepared for the walk I was on.
I stepped through storms with no armor,
hoping not to sink when the winds picked up.
And they always picked up.
But God—
He met me barefoot.
And instead of handing me shoes,
He toughened my feet.
I learned to walk through rejection,
to press through misunderstanding,
to run toward purpose even when the road was gravel.
He didn't always remove the pain—
Sometimes He repurposed it.
He used it to make me bold,
so that I could look back and say,
"That didn't break me. That built me."

I WENT FROM CRYING in parking lots,
    to praying in cars.
    From feeling forgotten,

TO REALIZING I WAS chosen.
    See, I used to want to prove myself.
    Now, I just want to please Him.
    Every night I slept in my car,
    every time I packed up my daughter's things
    not knowing when I'd see her again,
    every memory that hurt more than healed—
    God turned each one into bricks under my feet.
    Now I walk taller.
    Not because life got easier—
    but because my faith got stronger.
    I'm not afraid to be seen anymore.
    Not afraid to be misunderstood.
    Not afraid to walk alone—
    because I'm never alone.
    He goes before me.
    He walks with me.
    He guards behind me.
    If you saw where I started,
    you'd understand why I shout.
    If you knew what I survived,
    you'd know why I write.
    If you could feel what I feel now—
    you'd believe in miracles.
    Because this girl once walked barefoot,
    and now she walks bold.

King James Version (KJV):
"He makes my feet like hinds' feet,
and sets me upon my high places."
Psalm 18:33 (KJV)

Chapter Forty-One:

"Full Bloom"

There comes a time in every garden when the flower that's been buried the longest finally breaks through.

That's me. That's this chapter.

I've waited, pressed, cried, endured, believed—sometimes barely.

But now...

I'm blooming.

Not because life got easier,

but because I refused to stay buried in the dirt people threw over me.

I didn't always see it coming.

There were so many "almosts"—

almost gave up,

almost turned back,

almost let go.

But God.

He saw the seed.

He saw the root.

And when others walked away,

He whispered,

"Grow anyway."

I used to wonder if I was too broken to be chosen,

too lost to be found, unworthy to be used, too late to rise.

But I've come to realize:

SCARS DON'T DISQUALIFY you—they identify you.

They mark what you made it through.
Now I walk with power.
Quiet, steady, undeniable power.
Not because of who I am,
but because of who He is in me.
I don't owe explanations for the dirt I came through.
It fertilized me.
It shaped me.
It made me resilient.
I am no longer surviving.
I am living.
No longer just hoping.
I am harvesting.
No longer just praying.
I am praising.
This is not the end of the story.
This is the chapter where everything starts making sense.
Where beauty rises from the ashes,
and favor falls like spring rain.
Where everything I lost becomes the testimony of what I gained in God.
And guess what?
It's still just the beginning.

Because full bloom doesn't mean the journey ends—
it means I'm finally standing in the sunlight God spoke over me before I was born.

King James Version (KJV):
"The wilderness and the solitary place shall be glad for them;
and the desert shall rejoice,
and blossom as the rose."
Isaiah 35:1 (KJV)

The Conclusion of The Healing of Harms

IF YOU'RE HOLDING THIS book, know this:
God is not finished with you.
Your story is still unfolding.
Every scar, every ache, every tear has meaning.
Your breath still holds purpose.
And the Author of life always writes the best endings—
even when the chapters feel dark.
I don't have all the answers,
but I know the One who does.
And with that knowledge, I step forward—
not with shame,
but with strength.
This isn't the end of my story.
It's the beginning of everything God promised me.
I was broken, but now I build.
As I continue to grow and walk in what He's revealing,
I'm learning to recognize the gifts He's placed within me—
and within all of us.
What once felt like ruins is becoming a strong foundation.
What I thought was the end was actually a divine beginning.
God is establishing me, just as He said He would.
And this journey? It's far from over.
There's more to say.
More to uncover.
More proof that His hand has been in every detail.

So stay with me—
the story continues.
And I believe it will stir your soul and remind you
that God truly finishes what He starts.
This next chapter is unplanned—
a shot in the dark—
but it's filled with light.
I've been given a chance I didn't expect,
and I'm leaning in with full surrender.
As any mother would,
I fought with everything I had to be reunited with my child.
I traveled across the U.S., heart in hand,
walking by faith, not sight.
I didn't get here by accident.
And I'm not turning back.

      King James Version (KJV):
    "And if thy right eye offends thee,
     pluck it out, and cast it from thee:
for it is profitable for thee that one of thy members should perish,
   and not that thy whole body should be cast into hell."
       Matthew 5:29 (KJV)

This is a holy rebuilding.

About the Author

Destiny Parsons writes with fire in her bones and faith in her heart. A survivor of storms, setbacks, and silence, she found her voice through healing—and now uses it to help others find theirs. Her stories are raw, real, and rooted in the belief that no pain is wasted when placed in God's hands. This story is where faith meets grit and purpose is born from pressure.

She dedicates her journey to her daughters—one a heavenly light, and one a living miracle—and to anyone who's ever been counted out but chose to rise anyway.

Read more at www.destinyparsons.com.

www.ingramcontent.com/pod-product-compliance
Lightning Source LLC
Chambersburg PA
CBHW050114170426
43198CB00014B/2569